HELLO, BODY! KIDNEYS

By Joyce Markovics

CHERRY LAKE PRESS
Ann Arbor, Michigan

CHERRY LAKE PRESS

Published in the United States of America by Cherry Lake Publishing Group
Ann Arbor, Michigan
www.cherrylakepublishing.com

Reading Adviser: Beth Walker Gambro, MS Ed., Reading Consultant, Yorkville, IL
Content Advisers: Sharon Markovics, MD, and Peter Markovics, MD
Book Designer: Ed Morgan

Photo Credits: freepik.com, 4; freepik.com, 5; © chaiyawat chaidet/Shutterstock, 6; freepik.com, 7; freepik.com, 8; freepik.com, 9; © Kletr/Shutterstock, 10; freepik.com, 11; © crystal light/Shutterstock, 12–13; © Pan Xunbin/Shutterstock, 13 top; freepik.com, 14; freepik.com, 16; freepik.com, 17; freepik.com, 18; freepik.com, 19; freepik.com, 20; © Suttha Burawonk/Shutterstock, 21.

Cherry Lake Press is an imprint of Cherry Lake Publishing Group.

Library of Congress Cataloging-in-Publication Data

Names: Markovics, Joyce L., author.
Title: Kidneys / by Joyce Markovics.
Description: Ann Arbor, Michigan : Cherry Lake Publishing, [2023] | Series:
   Hello, body! | Includes bibliographical references and index. |
   Audience: Grades 4-6
Identifiers: LCCN 2022003693 (print) | LCCN 2022003694 (ebook) | ISBN
   9781668909614 (hardcover) | ISBN 9781668911211 (paperback) | ISBN
   9781668914397 (pdf) | ISBN 9781668912805 (ebook)
Subjects: LCSH: Kidneys—Juvenile literature.
Classification: LCC QP249 .M36 2023 (print) | LCC QP249 (ebook) | DDC
   612.4/63—dc23/eng/20220228
LC record available at https://lccn.loc.gov/2022003693
LC ebook record available at https://lccn.loc.gov/2022003694

Printed in the United States of America by
Corporate Graphics

CONTENTS

A PERFECT MATCH

In September 2020, Reid Alexander and Rafael Díaz started dating. A few weeks later, Reid's kidneys began to fail. Rafael did everything he could to help Reid. He stayed at the hospital with him and drove him to the doctor. The couple grew even closer. Reid knew that he wanted to share his life with Rafael.

By the time Reid and Rafael got married in April, Reid's kidneys were barely working. He needed a kidney **transplant**. To see if Rafael could **donate** one of his healthy kidneys to Reid, doctors tested his blood. They needed to make sure his kidney was a good match for Reid's. Luckily, it was!

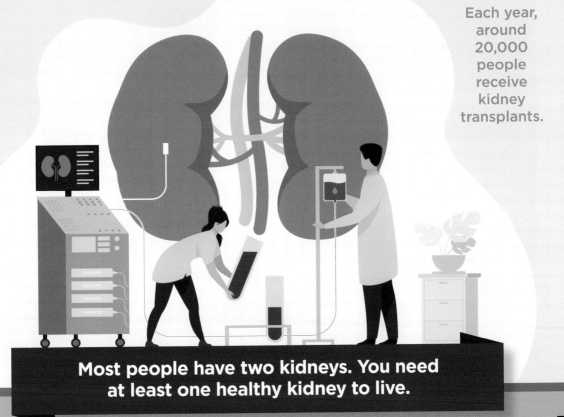

Each year, around 20,000 people receive kidney transplants.

Most people have two kidneys. You need at least one healthy kidney to live.

Rafael was thrilled he could help save his husband's life. It's amazing to "give someone else the opportunity to live," Rafael said. In August 2021, doctors removed one of Rafael's kidneys. They transplanted it into Reid. The surgery was a success. "It's crazy how fast I feel I recovered," Reid said.

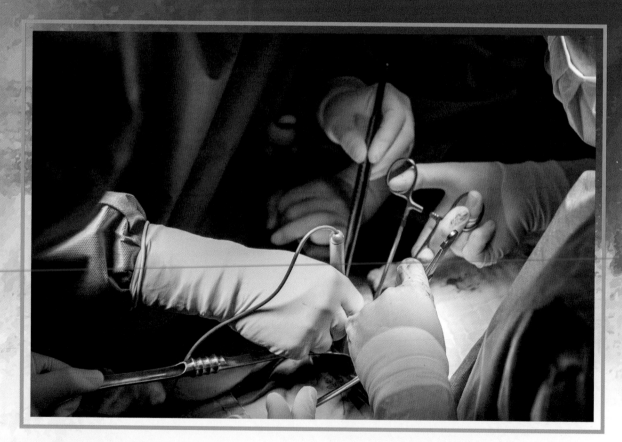

These doctors are performing a kidney transplant. The operation takes about 4 hours.

"It was the best experience in our life," said Rafael after the surgery. Reid added, "It'll definitely strengthen our bond." As it turns out, Reid and Rafael are a perfect match—in more ways than one.

KIDNEY FACTS

Your kidneys are amazing organs. They're tucked deep inside your body beneath your rib cage. Place your hands on your lower back. You *can't* feel your kidneys, but that's where they are! Now hold up your hand and make a fist. That's about how big one kidney is.

The kidneys have a few important jobs. One is to remove waste from your blood. They're kind of like the body's garbage collectors. So how does waste get in your blood in the first place?

It's no surprise that your kidneys look a lot like kidney beans!

Blood carries nutrients around your body. Your body breaks down these nutrients. In the process, waste is created. Waste includes salts, **calcium**, and certain **chemicals**. This is when the kidneys jump into action. They balance the chemicals and water in the blood. They remove any waste, along with the extra water that your body doesn't need.

Your kidneys keep your body in a state of balance called homeostasis (hoh-mee-oh-STAY-sus).

To get to your kidneys, your blood travels through the renal **arteries**. These are two big blood vessels. On average, humans have over 1 gallon (3.8 liters) of blood moving through their bodies. Your kidneys filter that amount of blood 40 times per day!

The renal arteries

The word *renal* relates to anything having to do with the kidneys.

Each kidney has an outer layer called a cortex. The cortex contains tiny parts known as nephrons (NEH-fronz). They filter the waste out of your blood. In the center of the kidney is the medulla. It's packed with cone-shaped **tissues** called pyramids. The pyramids further filter the blood. The result of all this filtering is a liquid waste product called urine (YOOR-uhn)—also known as pee!

CORTEX

MEDULLA

An extreme
close-up of
kidney tissue

**If you look inside a kidney with a powerful microscope,
you would see more than 1 million nephrons.**

GOT TO GO!

Once the kidneys make urine, it travels down a long tube. This tube is called a ureter (YOOR-uh-tuhr). Each kidney has one. Then the urine collects in a soft, stretchy sac called the bladder.

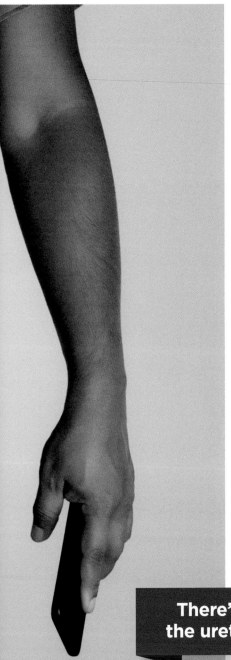

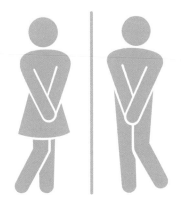

When your bladder is about half full, you might feel pressure in your belly. That's your body telling your brain: "It's time to go to the bathroom!" Finally, when you pee, the urine moves from your bladder to the **urethra** and passes out of your body.

Together, your kidneys, ureters, bladder, and urethra make up the urinary system.

There's a ring of muscle between the bladder and the urethra. Only when it relaxes can you pass urine.

That's not all your kidneys do. They also produce chemicals called hormones. One hormone made by the kidneys tells your body to make red blood cells.

Red blood cells carry oxygen in your blood. The kidneys keep your bones healthy too!

The kidneys also help control the pressure of blood inside your blood vessels.

Kidneys also help the body stay balanced. For example, your body needs a certain level of fluids and minerals to be healthy. What's amazing is your kidneys control these levels automatically. For example, if you're **dehydrated**, your kidneys hold onto more fluids. If you drink a lot, you release more fluids!

Sometimes, your urine might appear darker in color. This can happen when you don't drink enough water or if you sweat a lot. That's your kidneys at work! If you notice your urine is dark yellow, grab a tall glass of water.

Sometimes, your doctor might ask you to provide a urine sample. Your urine can tell the doctor how well your kidneys are working.

So why is urine yellow? The yellow color comes from urochrome (YOOR-uh-krohm). Your body produces this yellowish chemical when it breaks down dead blood cells. Your urine also contains **urea**, **ammonia**, **creatinine**, and other chemicals. But mostly, urine is made of water.

KIDNEY PROBLEMS

There are many **diseases** that can affect the kidneys. Sometimes, minerals in your urine build up and form **crystals**. Over time, they can become hard stones in the kidneys. Often, they pass on their own. Larger kidney stones can reduce or stop the flow of urine. These require immediate treatment.

Pain in a person's lower back can indicate kidney issues.

Kidney stones can be as tiny as a grain of sand or much larger.

Doctors called nephrologists (nih-FRAH-luh-jists) treat kidney diseases and help keep the kidneys healthy. Just like your brain and heart, you also need your kidneys—at least one—to live!

The biggest kidney stone ever discovered was 5 inches (13 centimeters) wide! That's about as big as a grapefruit. It had to be removed by a surgeon.

Here are some ways to keep your kidneys healthy:

- Drink plenty of water! Your kidneys need plenty of water to function well.

- Urinate when you need to. Holding urine in your bladder for too long isn't healthy.

- After using the toilet, always wipe from front to back. Getting bacteria from your backside into your urethra can lead to a painful urinary tract infection (UTI).

GLOSSARY

ammonia (uh-MOHN-yuh) colorless gas with a strong smell

arteries (AHR-tuh-reez) blood vessels that travel from the heart to the rest of the body

bacteria (bak-TEER-ee-uh) tiny living things; some bacteria are helpful, while others can cause disease

calcium (KAL-see-uhm) a chemical found mainly in bones and teeth

chemicals (KEH-muh-kuhlz) natural substances that help the body function

creatinine (kree-AH-tuh-neen) a chemical found in urine, blood, and muscle

crystals (KRISS-tuhlz) special kinds of solid materials that form a repeating pattern

dehydrated (dee-HYE-dray-tid) not having enough water in a person's body

diseases (duh-ZEE-zez) illnesses

donate (DOH-nayt) to give something away

surgeon (SUR-juhn) a doctor who performs operations

tissues (TISH-ooz) groups of similar cells that form a part of or an organ in the body

transplant (trans-PLANT) to take a body part from one person and place it in another

urea (yoo-REE-uh) a chemical that's found in urine

urethra (yoo-REE-thruh) the tube that carries urine from the body out of the body

FIND OUT MORE

BOOKS

Gold, Susan Dudley. *Learning About the Digestive and Excretory Systems*. Berkeley Heights, NJ: Enslow Publishers, 2013.

Simon, Seymour. *The Human Body*. New York, NY: HarperCollins, 2008.

Spilsbury, Louise. *Digestion and Excretion*. Chicago, IL: Heinemann Raintree, 2008.

WEBSITES

Britannica Kids: Kidney
https://kids.britannica.com/students/article/kidney/275267

KidsHealth: Urinary System
https://kidshealth.org/en/kids/usmovie.html

National Kidney Foundation: All About Kidneys
https://www.kidney.org/atoz/content/all-about-kidneys-basics-kids

INDEX

ABOUT THE AUTHOR

Joyce Markovics has written hundreds of books for kids. She marvels at the human body—and all the things we still don't know about it. She dedicates this book to anyone who has donated an organ or is willing to. Thank you!